Knowles Shaw

Sparkling jewels for the Sunday school

A new collection of choice music

Knowles Shaw

Sparkling jewels for the Sunday school
A new collection of choice music

ISBN/EAN: 9783337135713

Printed in Europe, USA, Canada, Australia, Japan

Cover: Foto ©Thomas Meinert / pixelio.de

More available books at **www.hansebooks.com**

FOR THE

SUNDAY SCHOOL.

A NEW

COLLECTION OF CHOICE MUSIC.

BY

KNOWLES SHAW.

CINCINNATI:
PUBLISHED BY JOHN CHURCH & CO.,
66 WEST FOURTH STREET.

PREFACE.

THE great success that has attended our former Sunday School Book, "SHINING PEARLS," and its wide-spread circulation, has encouraged the Author to contribute these "SPARKLING JEWELS" to the cause of Sunday Schools.

In this work will be found more than one hundred of the choicest gems, sparkling with living truth, fresh from the richest mines.

Many of these "JEWELS" of song have been composed especially for this work, and never appeared before; others gathered from the very best authors; and none have been admitted except such as breathe a pure gospel sentiment, uncontaminated by any light or unhallowed associations.

The music is easy, and well adapted to the hymns and songs, and may be used in Sunday Schools, Social Meetings, or in the Family Circle.

All contributors to this work have been duly credited where their compositions appear, but we would here render them our sincere thanks for the same.

We now send forth this little book on its mission; and sincerely hope, and most earnestly pray, that it may awaken in the minds of all, the love of living truth, and be instrumental in leading many early to seek the Lord, that they may be found among his "JEWELS" when he comes, and finally "Gather 'round the Great White Throne" "Over there," "Far beyond" this world of sorrow, to "Praise the Lord" forever.

KNOWLES SHAW.

Every piece in this work is copyright property, and no person, therefore, has the right to use either poetry or music, without permission.

Entered, according to Act of Congress, in the year 1871, by
JOHN CHURCH & CO.,
In the Office of the Librarian of Congress, at Washington, D. C.

ELECTROTYPED AT THE FRANKLIN TYPE FOUNDRY, CINCINNATI.

3 They are going, only going
　Out of pain, and into bliss;
　Out of sad and sinful weakness
　　Into perfect holiness.
　Snowy brows—no care shall shade them;
　Bright eyes—tears shall never dim;
　Rosy lips—no time shall fade them;
　　Jesus called them unto him.
　　　Going home, etc.

4 Little hearts, forever stainless;
　Little hands as pure as they
　Little feet, by angels guided
　　In a pure and perfect way:
　They are going, ever going,
　Leaving many a lonely spot;
　But 't is Jesus who has called them,
　　Suffer and forbid them not.
　　　Going home, etc.

THE LAMBS OF THE UPPER FOLD.

"Suffer the little children to come unto me, and forbid them not, for of such is the kingdom of heaven."

Words and Music by K. Shaw.

Tenderly.

1. Man-y children dear to us while here Have gone, but we are told That our ab-sent ones in heaven ap-pear, A-mong the saints en-shore; As the lambs of the up-per fold.

2. I see the throng, I hear the song, 'Mid the angels on the oth-er shore; In the pastures green they are ev-er seen, On Ca-naan's peace-ful rolled, In the land where they weep no more.

Chorus.

For Je-sus leads the ten-der lambs, They are now in the land where they ne'er grow old; How dear to us are the lov-ing lambs, The lambs of the up-per fold.

2 Now let us live—to Jesus give
  Our strength while young and old;
  So when we are gone we may rest at home,
  And walk the streets of gold,
  With the lambs of the upper fold.
    For Jesus leads, etc.

4 Then let us go to the land above,
  And be with the saints enrolled,
  To bear the palm, and wear the crown,
  And share that bliss untold,
  With the lambs of the upper fold.
    For Jesus leads, etc.

WE'LL STAND THE STORM.*

Words by Amy Arnott.
L. Vese.

1. How bravely sails the gallant ship, And thro' the tempest rides;
2. By rudest gales and roughest waves, Still onward she is driven;

Her wings of canvas all outspread, And like a bird she flies.
And fears no danger while she finds They're bearing her to heaven.

f Chorus.
We'll stand the storm, 't will not be long, We'll anchor by and by!
We'll stand the storm, 't will not be long, We'll anchor by and by.

3 The Christian sails a stormy sea,
By angry billows tossed;
With Jesus ever in command,
He knows he'll not be lost.
We'll stand, etc.

4 We'll trust him when the days are dark,
And when the tempests roar;
For he will guide our vessel safe
To yonder blissful shore.
We'll stand, etc.

*From "Silver Wings," published by O. Ditson & Co., Boston, Mass., by permission.

COME TO ME.

Words from the "Child's Paper." J. H. Rosecrans.

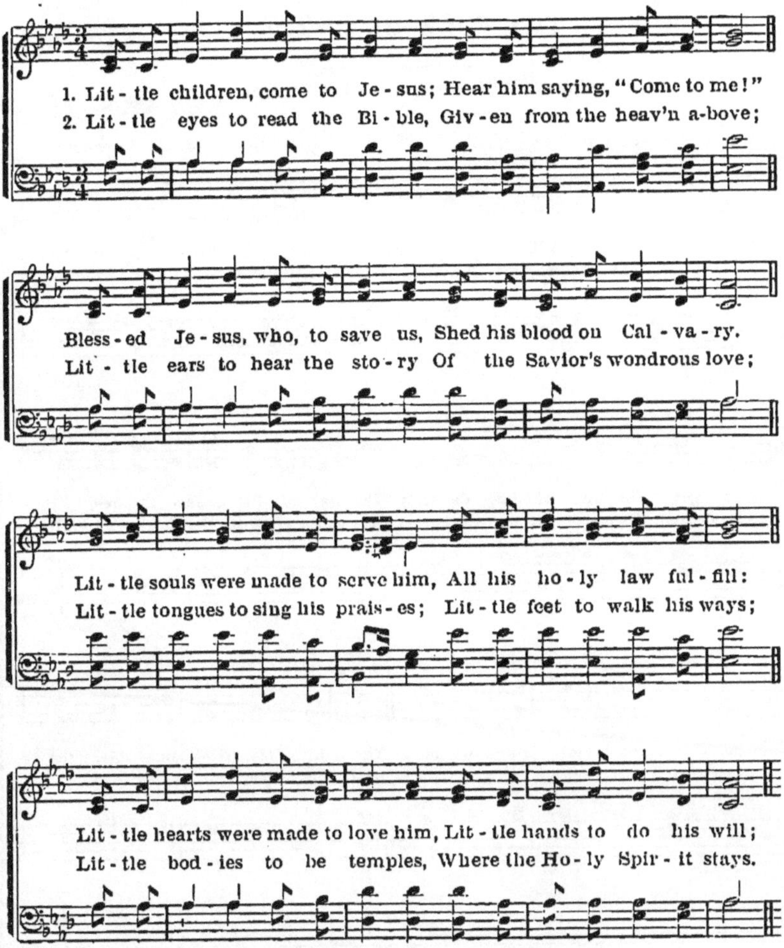

1. Lit-tle children, come to Je-sus; Hear him saying, "Come to me!"
   Bless-ed Je-sus, who, to save us, Shed his blood on Cal-va-ry.
   Lit-tle souls were made to serve him, All his ho-ly law ful-fill:
   Lit-tle hearts were made to love him, Lit-tle hands to do his will;

2. Lit-tle eyes to read the Bi-ble, Giv-en from the heav'n a-bove;
   Lit-tle ears to hear the sto-ry Of the Savior's wondrous love;
   Lit-tle tongues to sing his prais-es; Lit-tle feet to walk his ways;
   Lit-tle bod-ies to be temples, Where the Ho-ly Spir-it stays.

3 There are little crowns in heaven,
  There are little harps of gold;
  There are little shining dresses,
  There are gems and joys untold.
  Jesus gave his blood to buy them;
  He has bought enough for all;
  Little children, come to Jesus—
  He has love for great and small.

THE BOOK OF BOOKS.*

"The word of our God shall stand forever."

Words by FANNY CHURCH. J. H. ROSECRANS.

1. The book of books, the Bi - ble, Oh, guard and keep it well, To all its sa - cred pa - ges, The way of life do tell; The way of life to each 'tis free, Yes, Je - sus died for you and me. The Bi - ble, the Bi - ble, the book of love and truth, Staff for a - ged pil-grims, guide for bounding youth.

2. Read from that o - pen volume, The words your heart will move, Of all God's ten - der kind-ness, His more than mor - tal love; Dear words of truth, they never fail, They reach to that with-in the vale. The Bi - ble, etc.

3 The lessons that it teaches,
   Are love to all mankind,
   Humility and mercy,
   In union sweet combined;
   Dear lessons of the boundless grace,
   That meets the darkest sinner's case.

4 Then keep that faithful teacher,
   Its precepts wise obey,
   And by and by you'll enter
   The Kingdom of the day;
   Then joy for thee, thy work is done,
   Thy Savior speaks the great "Well done!"

*From "Little Sower," by permission.

THE BANNER OF HIS LOVE.

Music by K. SHAW.

Spirited, but not too fast.

1. Ye wretched, hun-gry, starving poor, Be-hold a roy-al feast;
2. See, Je-sus stands with o-pen arms, He calls, he bids you come;

Where mer-cy spreads her bounteous store For ev'-ry humble guest.
Guilt holds you back, and fear alarms, But see, there yet is room.

Chorus.

Come, join in the army of the Lord; Come, join in the army of the Lord; In the

army of the Lord, 'Neath the banner of his love, Come, join in the army of the Lord.

3 Room in the Savior's bleeding heart,
  There love and pity meet;
  Nor will he bid the soul depart
  That trembles at his feet.
    Come, join, etc.

4 O, come, and with his children taste
  The blessings of his love,
  While hope attends the sweet repast
  Of nobler joys above.
    Come, join, etc.

5 There, with united hearts and voice,
  Before the eternal throne,
  Ten thousand thousand souls rejoice
  In ecstasies unknown.
    Come, join, etc.

6 And yet ten thousand thousand more
  Are welcome still to come;
  Ye longing souls, the grace adore,
  Approach, there yet is room.
    Come, join, etc.

PRECIOUS TREASURE.

"Thy word is Truth."—*John* xvii: 17.

Music by K. SHAW.

1. Ho-ly Bi-ble! book di-vine! Pre-cious treas-ure! thou art mine;
2. Mine to chide me when I rove; Mine to show a Sav-ior's love;

Mine to tell me whence I came; Mine to teach me what I am.
Mine thou art to guide and guard; Mine to pun-ish or re-ward.

Chorus.

Ho-ly Bi-ble! book di-vine! Ho-ly Bi-ble! book di-vine!

Pre-cious treas-ure! thou art mine! Pre-cious treas-ure! thou art mine!

3 Mine to comfort in distress,
Suffering in this wilderness;
Mine to show, by living faith,
Man can triumph over death.
    Holy Bible, etc.

4 Mine to tell of joys to come,
And the rebel sinner's doom;
O, thou holy book divine!
Precious treasure! thou art mine!
    Holy Bible, etc.

STAND UP FOR JESUS.*

Words by THETA.
mf Boldly.

1. Stand up for Je-sus! let not pride Keep thee away from him who died
2. Stand up for Je-sus! let not fear Cause thee to shrink when danger's near;
3. Stand up for Je-sus! let not shame Make thee deny his bles-sed name;

To save thy soul; but to the fight Go forth in thy great Captain's might.
Je-ho-vah's arm will thee uphold, His grace can make the faint heart bold.
The on-ly name that God has giv'n By which lost men may en-ter heaven.

ff Chorus.

Stand up for Je-sus! yea, stand fast! Con-quer or die—the conflict past,

Him that o'ercometh he will own, And place the vic-tor near his throne.

4 Stand up for Jesus! let not love
To this vain world, thy purpose move:
Forsaking all earth's empty toys,
Keep thine eye fixed on heavenly joys.
    Stand up for Jesus, etc.

5 Stand up for Jesus! let not sin
Defile thy soul, but strive to win
The crown of righteousness, prepared
For those who fear and serve the Lord.
    Stand up for Jesus, etc.

* From "Silver Wings," published by O. Ditson & Co., Boston, Mass., by permission.

WAIT A LITTLE LONGER.

"Wait on the Lord."

Words and Music by K. Shaw.

3 Work for Jesus while 't is day,
    Work a little longer;
  Sow, and faint not by the way,
    Work a little longer.
  Think not that you work in vain;
  Soon you'll reap the golden grain,
  On yon bright celestial plain;
    Then, wait a little longer.

4 Should your tears oft freely flow,
    Wait a little longer;
  Jesus wept while here below,
    Wait a little longer.
  Soon we'll walk the golden street;
  Soon, the parted here, will meet;
  Soon we'll bow at Jesus' feet;
    Then, wait a little longer.

GARLANDS WE BRING.

From "The Song Garland." Words and Music by J. Wm. Suffern.

1. Gar-lands we bring, fresh garlands of song, To welcome our Sa-vior and King,
   sing of the Sa-vior's ten - der love, And mercies so gra-cious-ly given,
2. Gar-lands we bring, fresh garlands of song, To Je-sus the praise all be given;
   join with the lov-ing an - gel band, And with them our voic - es blend,

Let's join our glad voic-es with the throng Of an-gels as they sing, They
By . . . .
For he it was said "Oh, let them come," There's children now in heaven, We'll
And . . . .

him who now reigns o'er all a-bove, O'er earth and o'er sea and heaven.
with them we'll shout all glo - ry be To Je-sus, the sin-ner's friend.

Chorus.

Wafting a - long sweet gar-lands of song,

Waft-ing sweet gar-lands of song,

O - ver the land and o - ver the sea,

O - ver the land and sea,

Sing-ing for Je-sus, Yes, sing-ing for Je-sus our theme shall be.

JESUS BY THE SEA.

Geo. F. Root. By permission.

Reverentially.

1. O, I love to think of Jesus as he sat beside the sea, Where the waves were only murm'ring on the strand, When he sat within the boat, on the silver wave afloat, While he taught the waiting people on the land.
2. O, I love to think of Jesus as he walked upon the sea, When the waves were rolling fearfully and grand, How the winds and waves were still, at the bidding of his will, While he brought his loved disciples safe to land.
3. O, I love to think of Jesus as he walked beside the sea, Where the fishers spread their nets upon the shore, How he bade them follow him, and for sake the paths of sin, And to be his true disciples evermore.

Chorus.

O! I love to think of Jesus by the sea; O! I love to think of Jesus by the sea, And I love the precious Word, Which he spake to them that heard, While he taught the waiting people by the sea.

O! I love to think of Jesus by the sea; O! I love to think of Jesus by the sea, How he walked upon the wave, His loved ones to save, While he brought them safely o'er the stormy sea.

O! I love to think of Jesus by the sea; O! I love to think of Jesus by the sea, And I long to leave my all, At the dear Redeemer's call, And his true disciple evermore to be.

"I SOON SHALL GO."

Words by "IDA."   W. H. DOANE.

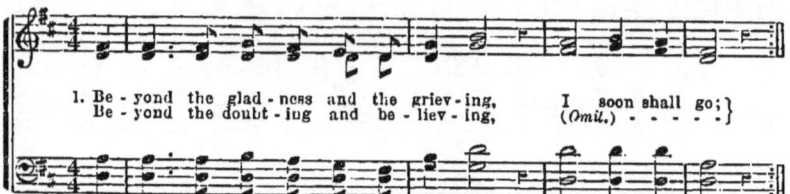

1. Be - yond the glad - ness and the griev - ing,
Be - yond the doubt - ing and be - liev - ing,   I soon shall go; (*Omit.*)

Be-yond the giv-ing and re - ceiv - ing, I soon shall go. My hap-py home,

Dear, dear home; In that land with the angel band, I'll find my heavenly home;

In that land with the an - gel band, I'll find my heavenly home.

2 Beyond the tempting and the warning,
   I soon shall go;
Beyond the loving and the scorning,
Beyond the darkness and the dawning,
   I soon shall go.
   My happy home,
   Dear, dear home;
In that land, with the angel band,
I'll find my heavenly home.

3 Beyond the smiling and the sighing,
   I soon shall go;
Beyond the hoping and the crying,
Beyond the living and the dying,
   I soon shall go.
   My happy home,
   Dear, dear home;
In that land, with the angel band,
I'll find my heavenly home.

MINE THE CROSS.

"If we suffer with him."—ROM. viii: 17.

Words by FANNY CROSBY.   From "Songs of Salvation," T. E. PERKINS, by per.

1. Mine the cross, and thine the glo-ry, Thou hast suffered once for me;
2. All I am thy grace has made me, All I am I owe to thee;

Let my life be calm or cloud-ed, I can trust it, Lord, to thee.
I can on-ly thank and praise thee For a love so pure and free.

Let me feel the sweet as-sur-ance Of thy pres-ence al-ways near;
I would dai-ly strive to fol-low Where thy blessed feet have led;

Grant me on-ly this, my Fa-ther, And my soul can nev-er fear.
May I fol-low, dai-ly grow-ing Up to thee, my liv-ing head.

3 Mine the cross, and thine the glory,
Thou hast borne it once for me;
Help me bear with Christian meekness
Every trial sent by thee.
On thy strength alone relying,
With thy lamp to cheer my way,
Leaning on the staff of mercy,
I will labor, trust, and pray.

3 Deeper, deeper grow the shadows;
Paler now the glowing west;
Swift the night of death advances;
Shall it be the night of rest?
Tarry with me, etc.

4 Tarry with me, O my Savior!
Lay my head upon thy breast
Till the morning; then awake me,
Morning of eternal rest.
Tarry with me, etc.

NEAR THE CROSS.

Words of last verse by K. S.
O. A. BARTHOLOMEW.

1. Near the cross our sta-tion ta-king, Earthly cares and joys forsak-ing; Meet it is for us to mourn; 'Twas for us he came from heaven, 'Twas for us his heart was riv-en; All his griefs for us were borne.

2. When no eye its pi-ty gave us, When there was no arm to save us, He his love and pow'r dis-played; By his stripes our help and heal-ing, By his death our life re-veal-ing, He for us the ran-som paid.

3 Jesus, may thy love constrain us,
That from sin we may refrain us,
In thy griefs may deeply grieve;
Thee our best affections giving,
To thy praise and honor living,
May we in thy glory live!

4 Then in realms of bliss and glory,
We will sing the wondrous story
Of our dear Redeemer's love,
And through ages still unceasing,
Joy, and bliss, and love increasing
In our blessed home above.

WAITING AT THE DOOR.

Words by Mrs. KATE M. REASONER. From "FRESH LEAVES," by per.

3 Many friends that traveled with me,
   Reached that portal long ago;
   One by one they left me battling
   With the dark and crafty foe.
   But they're watching, etc.

4 Yes, their pilgrimage was shorter,
   And their triumphs sooner won;
   Oh, how lovingly they'll greet me
   When the toils of life are done.
   For they're watching, etc.

5 Oh, how soon shall I be with them,
   And shall join their glorious throng;
   There to mingle in their worship,
   And to swell their mighty song.
   Yes, they're watching, etc.

6 Yet, O Lord, I wait thy pleasure,
   For thy time and ways are best;
   Hear me, Lord, for I am weary,
   O my Father, bid me rest.
   They are watching, etc.

ONWARD AND UPWARD.

"I press toward the mark for the prize."—PAUL.

Words by W. S. WINFIELD.   K. SHAW.

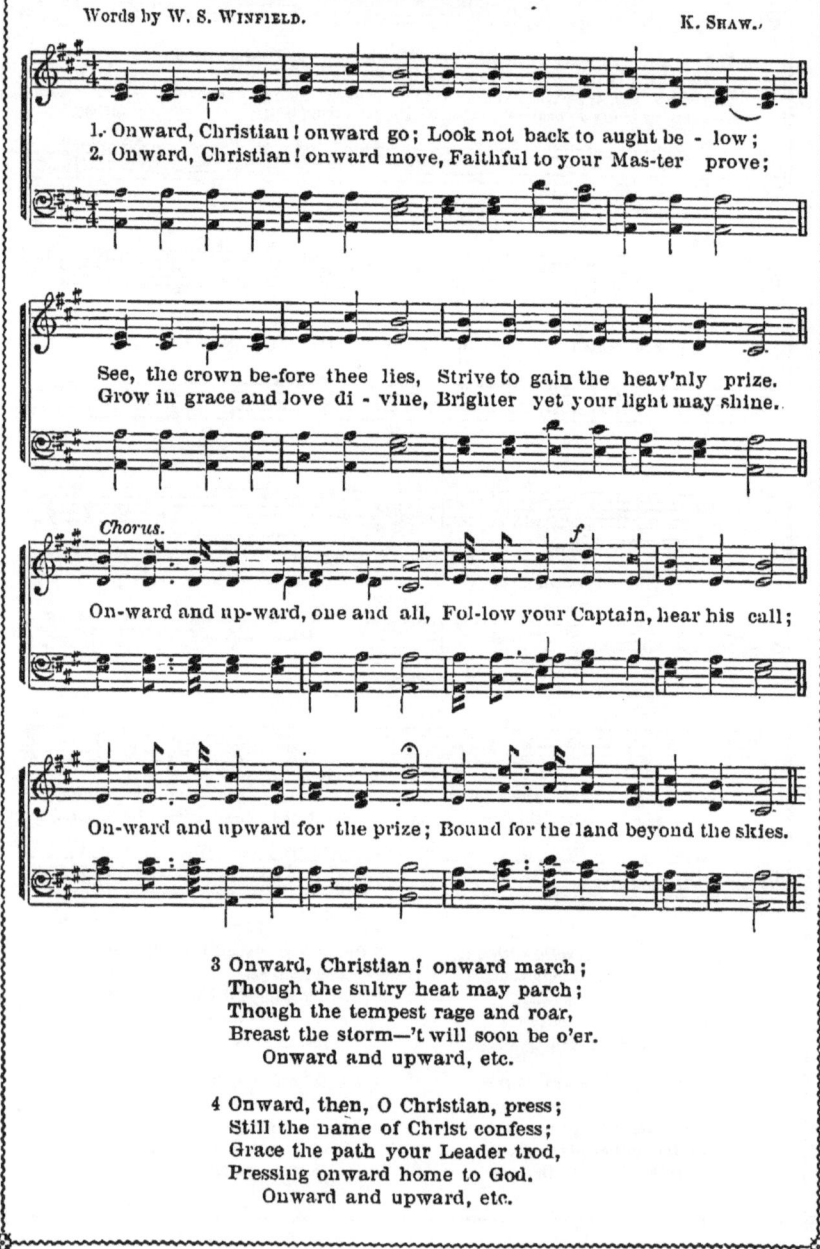

1. Onward, Christian! onward go; Look not back to aught be-low;
2. Onward, Christian! onward move, Faithful to your Mas-ter prove;

See, the crown be-fore thee lies, Strive to gain the heav'nly prize.
Grow in grace and love di-vine, Brighter yet your light may shine.

Chorus.

On-ward and up-ward, one and all, Fol-low your Captain, hear his call;

On-ward and upward for the prize; Bound for the land beyond the skies.

3 Onward, Christian! onward march;
Though the sultry heat may parch;
Though the tempest rage and roar,
Breast the storm—'t will soon be o'er.
Onward and upward, etc.

4 Onward, then, O Christian, press;
Still the name of Christ confess;
Grace the path your Leader trod,
Pressing onward home to God.
Onward and upward, etc.

MY BEAUTIFUL DREAM.

"THE CITY LIETH FOUR SQUARE."

"These are they who have come up through great tribulation, and have washed their robes in the blood of the Lamb."

Words and Music by H. SHAW.

Slowly and distinctly.

I dreamed of the land of the pure and bright, The city of God, the saint's delight,

And the saints of all ages, and children were there, That city of God, and that home to share.

Chorus.

O! that beau-ti-ful dream; O! that beau-ti-ful dream;

Shall I the saints, and those children see, Or shall it be on-ly a dream?

2 I dreamed that the trials of life were o'er,
And the saints were walking the golden shore;
Where they ate of the fruit of life's evergreen tree,
O! beautiful, beautiful dream to me.
  O! that beautiful dream, etc.

3 I dreamed that I saw them in robes of white;
With crowns on their brow of golden light;
I looked as they wandered life's river along,
I listened, and heard a most beautiful song.
  O! that beautiful dream, etc.

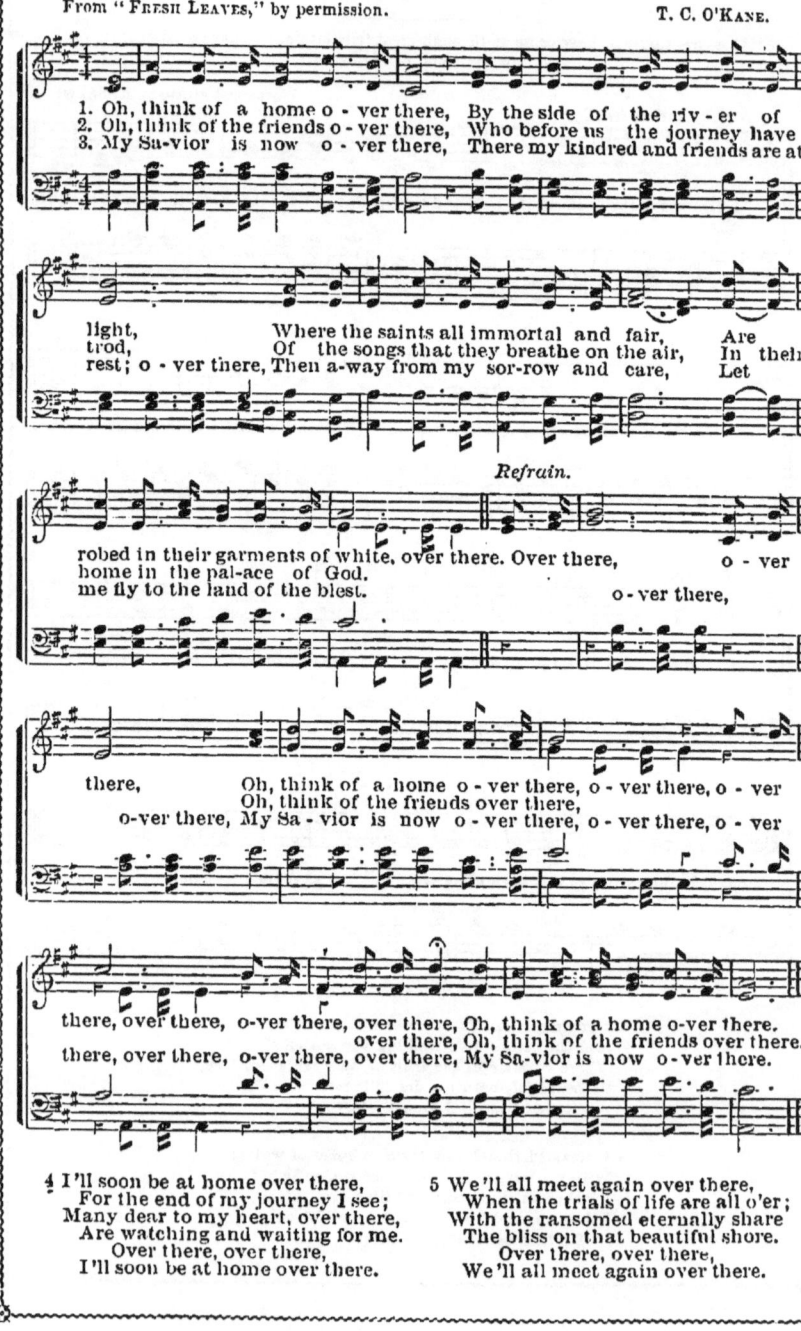

HOME OF THE SOUL.

"And there shall in nowise enter into it any thing that defileth."

From "SINGING PILGRIM" & "MUSICAL LEAVES," by permission.   PHILIP PHILLIPS.

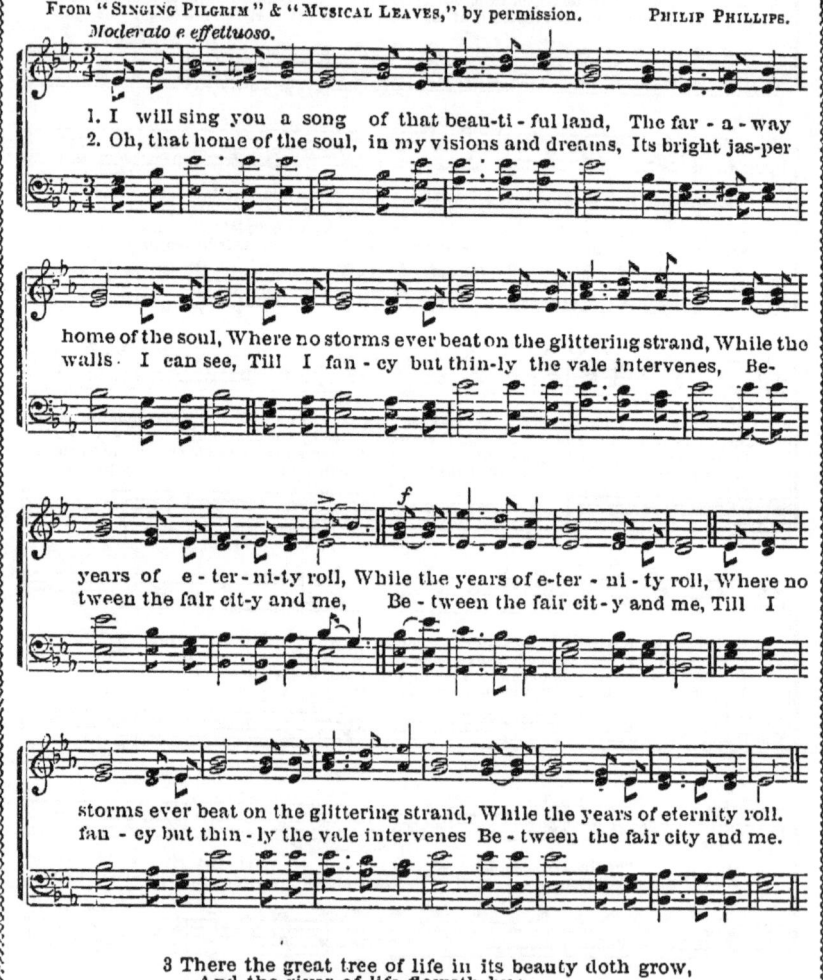

1. I will sing you a song of that beau-ti-ful land, The far-a-way home of the soul, Where no storms ever beat on the glittering strand, While the years of e-ter-ni-ty roll, While the years of e-ter-ni-ty roll, Where no storms ever beat on the glittering strand, While the years of eternity roll.

2. Oh, that home of the soul, in my visions and dreams, Its bright jasper walls I can see, Till I fan-cy but thin-ly the vale intervenes, Be-tween the fair cit-y and me, Be-tween the fair cit-y and me, Till I fan-cy but thin-ly the vale intervenes Be-tween the fair city and me.

3 There the great tree of life in its beauty doth grow,
   And the river of life floweth by;
   For no death ever enters that city, you know,
   And nothing that maketh a lie.

4 That unchangeable home is for you and for me,
   Where Jesus of Nazareth stands;
   The king of all kingdoms forever is he,
   And he holdeth our crowns in his hands.

5 Oh how sweet it will be in that beautiful land,
   So free from all sorrow and pain!
   With songs on our lips, and with harps in our hands,
   To meet one another again.

DENNIS.

1. Blest be the tie that binds Our hearts in Christian love; The fellowship of kindred minds Is like to that above.
2. Before our Father's throne, We pour our ardent prayers; Our fears, our hopes, our aims are one, Our comforts and our cares.

3 We share our mutual woes,
Our mutual burdens bear;
And often for each other flows,
The sympathizing tear.

4 When we asunder part,
It gives us inward pain;
But we shall still be joined in heart,
And hope to meet again.

CORONATION. C. M.

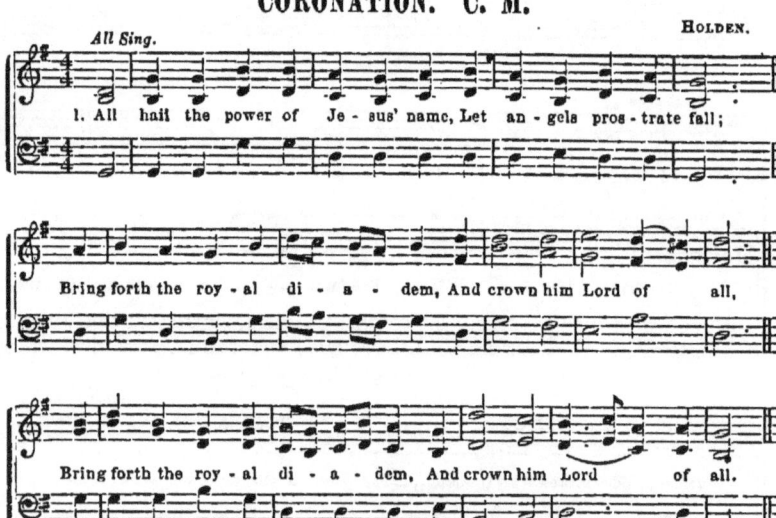

1. All hail the power of Jesus' name, Let angels prostrate fall; Bring forth the royal diadem, And crown him Lord of all, Bring forth the royal diadem, And crown him Lord of all.

2 You chosen seed of Israel's race,
A remnant weak and small,
Hail him who saves you by his grace,
And crown him Lord of all.
3 You Gentile sinners, ne'er forget
The wormwood and the gall;
Go, spread your trophies at his feet,
And crown him Lord of all.

4 Let every kindred, every tribe,
On this terrestrial ball,
To him all majesty ascribe,
And crown him Lord of all.
5 O, that with yonder sacred throng,
We at his feet may fall!
We'll join the everlasting song,
And crown him Lord of all.

4 Then come, brother pilgrims, let love freely flow,
As on to that beautiful home we shall go;
For Jesus has said we must go hand in hand,
If ever we enter that beautiful land.
  Oh, beautiful home, etc.

5 Oh, my soul is now weary of toiling below,
To the home of the purified saints would I go,
With Jesus, my Savior, forever to stand,
'Mid the shining ones of the better land.
  Oh, beautiful home, etc.

O, HAPPY PILGRIM.

Words by Mrs. M. A. KIDDER. Specially contributed to this work by W. H. DOANE.

1. O, blessed bond that makes us one, U-nit-ed in the Savior's love;
To Canaan's land we'll jour-ney on, Un-til we reach our home a-bove.

2. Though thorns may pierce our weary feet, Though heat may scorch, and cold may chill;
We still will sing our anthems sweet, And bold-ly march up Zi-on's hill.

Chorus.

O hap-py pil-grim, tell me true, To save my soul, what shall I do?
'Tis Christ a-lone can save from sin, And make us pure and white within.

3 O, brother pilgrim! look on high,
   Above the clouds, above the sun;
   The pearly gates are very nigh,
   Our toilsome work is almost done.
      O, happy pilgrim, etc.

4 O, blessed time, when we shall rise,
   Our trials o'er, our cares laid down;
   On angel pinions to the skies,
   And there receive the pilgrim's crown.
      O, happy pilgrim, etc.

TARRY NOT HERE.*

E. C. REVONS.

mf Cheerfully.

1. We are trav-el-ers here be-low, Onward, joyful-ly, still we go;
2. Oh, the light of that sky se-rene, Mor-tal vis-ion hath nev-er seen;

On-ly pil-grims here we roam; Je-sus will gath-er us home.
Strains no mor-tal ear can hear Ech-o for-ev-er there.

f Chorus.

On-ward! On-ward! Tar-ry not, tar-ry not here! On-ward to your heaven-ly home, Je-sus bids you welcome home. On-ward! Onward! Tarry not, tarry not here! Onward! Onward! Tarry not, tarry not here!

3 Come and join us, a pilgrim band,
  Going home to our Fatherland;
  Crowns of joy, divinely fair,
  Jesus will give us there.
    Onward, etc.

4 Going home to the fields of light,
  Going home to our mansions bright;
  Oh, how happy we shall be,
  Jesus there to see.
    Onward, etc.

* From "Silver Wings," published by O. Ditson & Co., Boston, Mass., by permission.

WHEN SHALL WE MEET AGAIN?

DR. L. MASON.

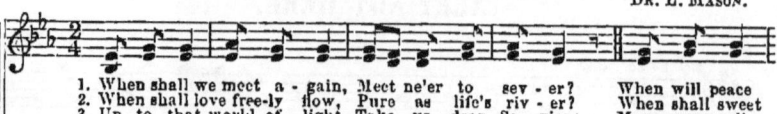

1. When shall we meet a-gain, Meet ne'er to sev-er? When will peace
2. When shall love free-ly flow, Pure as life's riv-er? When shall sweet
3. Up to that world of light, Take us, dear Sa-vior; May we all

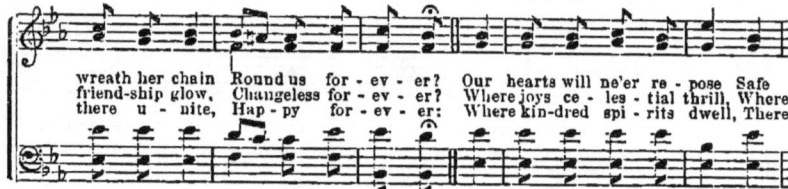

wreath her chain Round us for-ev-er? Our hearts will ne'er re-pose Safe
friend-ship glow, Changeless for-ev-er? Where joys ce-les-tial thrill, Where
there u-nite, Hap-py for-ev-er: Where kin-dred spi-rits dwell, There

from each blast that blows In this dark vale of woes— Nev-er—no, nev-er.
bliss each heart shall fill, And fears of part-ing chill Nev-er—no, nev-er.
may our mu-sic swell, And time our joys dis-pel, Nev-er—no, nev-er.

TO-DAY THE SAVIOR CALLS.

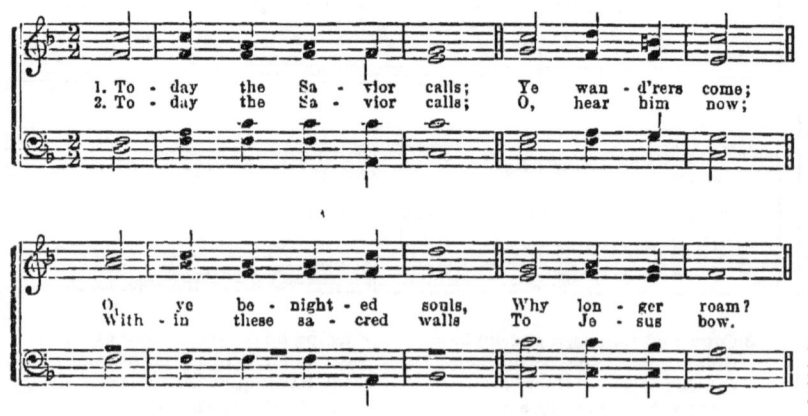

1. To-day the Sa-vior calls; Ye wan-d'rers come;
2. To-day the Sa-vior calls; O, hear him now;

O, ye be-night-ed souls, Why lon-ger roam?
With-in these sa-cred walls To Je-sus bow.

3 To day the Savior calls;
   For refuge fly;
   The storm of justice falls,
   And death is nigh.

4 The Spirit calls to-day;
   Yield to his power;
   O, grieve him not away;
   'T is mercy's hour.

WE'RE MARCHING ON.

(Temperance Song.)

Words from "YOUTH'S TEMPERANCE VISITOR." Contributed by J. H. ROSECRANS.

1. We're marching on! we're marching on! A lit-tle, loy-al band,

And want and woe, wher-e'er we go, Must van-ish from our land.
D. C. We'll keep it bright with faith by night, And glad by day with song.

{ For wine, and ale, and rum must fall, And al-co-hol must flee; }
{ We'll break the chain of vice in twain, And set the cap-tive free; }

For we're marching on! we're marching on! And tho' our way be long,

2 We're marching on! we're marching on!
 With courage calm and high,
And still above, with peace and love,
 Our conquering banners fly.
At last the hosts of wrong shall yield,
 The right shall reign at last;
For young and old we're bound to hold
 The temperance standard fast!

CHORUS.
For we're marching on! we're marching on!
 A little, loyal band;
Come woe or weal, with fervent zeal,
 Around our flag we'll stand.

3 We're marching on! we're marching on!
 We would not go alone;
We call on those, who hate our foes,
 To make our cause their own.
We call on those who love the truth,
 The children of the light,
With heart and hand to join the band,
 And battle for the right.

CHORUS.
For we're marching on! we're marching on!
 A little, loyal band;
Though death be near, we will not fear,
 The Lord will save our land.

3 Go, bearing the ensign of love,
　　Its glories forever unfurled;
　　Recruit for the army above,
　　Your warrant embraces the world.
　　We care not, etc.

THE RIVER OF DEATH.*

Words by FANNY CHURCH.   J. H. TENNEY.

1. Oh, bright is the shore that lies be-yond, And shining its gold-en sands are seen;
But fear-ful and dark, with stormy waves, The riv-er of Death rolls in be-tween.

2. Oh, fair are the hills that greet our sight, And clad in their robes of liv-ing green,
We trem-ble and turn, with tearful eyes, For the river of Death that rolls be-tween.

Chorus.
Oh, hap-py the chil-dren fair and sweet, That there on the Savior's bo-som lean;
He car-ried them safely thro' the waves Of the riv-er of Death that rolls between.

3 Oh, great is the throng of ransomed there,
   Whose souls have been washed from every sin;
  And why should we shrink and fear to pass
   The river of Death that rolls between?
    Oh, happy the children, etc.

4 Oh, sweet is the thought to fearful souls,
   That Christ through the waters dark hath been;
  His power to save will bring us through
   The river of Death that rolls between.
    Oh, happy the children, etc.

*From the "Little Sower," by permission.

OUR JOURNEY.*

Words by J. Pollard.
Karl Reden.

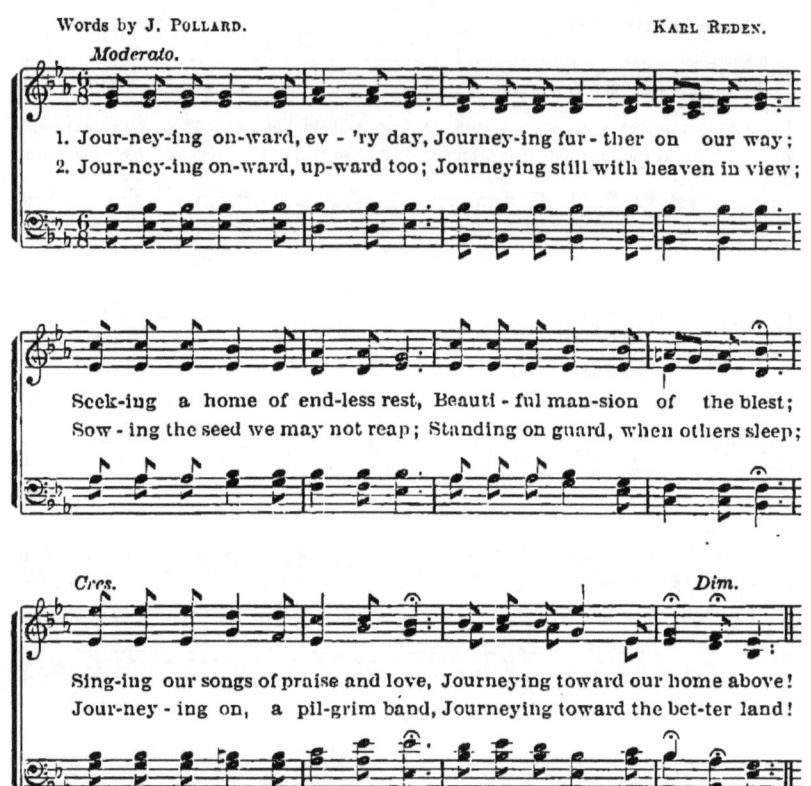

3 Journeying onward, hope shall cheer;
Journeying on, new joys appear!
Angels will guide the feet that stray,
Keeping them in the narrow way.
Hopefully waiting, trusting still,
Thus we may do our Master's will.

4 Journeying onward, oh, how sweet
Shall be the rest at Jesus' feet!
Then in the joys of saints we'll share;
Oh, may we meet each loved one there!
Soon shall our pilgrim days be o'er,
Then shall we sin and toil no more.

*From "Silver Wings," published by O. Ditson & Co., Boston, Mass., by permission.

HARVEST HOME.

"Cast thy bread upon the waters; for thou shalt find it after many days."— Eccl. xi: 1.

Rev. Alfred Taylor.   From "Songs of Salvation," T. E. Perkins, by per.

1. Cast thy bread up-on the wa - ters, Find it af - ter ma - ny days;
Je - sus' toil - ing sons and daugh - ters, Loud shall sing their har-vest praise.

2. Sow in faith, on God de - pend - ing, E'en in hard-est, poor - est soil;
Pa - tient care and la - bor spend - ing, God will re - com-pense the toil.

3. Sow in faith, nor ev - er wea - ry, Hop-ing on, and faint-ing not,
Tho' the day be dark and drear - y, Reap-ing soon shall be thy lot.

Chorus.
God's own chil - dren glad - ly sing - ing, Sing - ing songs of har - vest home;
Gold - en sheaves in tri - umph bring - ing, Je - sus bids us wel-come home.

     4 Soon shall cease the time of sowing,
        Soon the waiting days be o'er,
        Plenteous harvest, richly growing,
        For God's glory, evermore.
          God's own children, etc.

     5 Golden sheaves in triumph bringing,
        Jesus' reapers hasten home!
        Harvest welcome gladly singing,
        Jesus meets them as they come.
          God's own children, etc.

"IT IS I, BE NOT AFRAID."

Words arranged for this work. K. SHAW.

1. Tossed with rough winds and faint with fear, A - bove the tem - pest
2. 'Tis   I who led thy steps a - right; 'Tis I who gave the
3. These rag - ing winds, this surg - ing sea, Bear not a threat of

soft and clear, What cheer - ing ac - cents greet mine ear:
blind their sight; 'Tis   I, thy Lord, thy Life, thy Light.
wrath to thee; That storm has all been spent on   me.

pp Duet.   Chorus. *f*

"It   is   I, be not a - fraid," "It is I, be not a - fraid."

4 This bitter cup fear not to drink;
 I know it well—oh, do not shrink;
 I tasted it o'er Kedron's brink;
  "It is I; be not afraid," etc.

5 When on the other shore thy feet
 Shall rest 'mid thousand welcomes sweet,
 One well-known voice thy heart shall greet,
  "It is I; be not afraid," etc.

6 From out the dazzling majesty,
 He'll gently whisper, "Lov'st thou me?"
 'T was not in vain I died for thee,
  "It is I; be not afraid," etc.

4 There's a song in the valley of blessing, so sweet
That angels would fain join the strain—
As, with rapturous praises, we bow at his feet,
Crying, "Worthy the Lamb that was slain."
Oh, come to this valley, etc.

LIFE'S DREAM.

Words by LONGFELLOW.　　　　　　　　　　　　　O. A. BARTHOLOMEW.

1. A-las! how poor and lit-tle worth Are all those glitt'ring
2. Where is the strength that spurned de-cay, The step that rolled so

toys of earth, That lure us here! Dreams of a sleep that
light and gay, The heart's blithe tone? The strength is gone, the

death must break; A-las! be-fore it bids us wake, They dis-ap-pear.
step is slow, And joy grows wea-ri-ness and woe When age comes on.

3 Our birth is but a starting-place;
　Life is the running of the race,
　　And death the goal;
　There all those glittering toys are brought;
　That path alone, of all unsought,
　　Is found of all.

4 Oh, let the soul its slumbers break,
　Arouse its senses, and awake
　　To see how soon
　Life, like its glories, glides away,
　And the stern footsteps of decay
　　Come stealing on.

THE WATER OF LIFE.

Words by FANNY CHURCH.   From "Little Sower."   J. H. TENNEY.

1. Beside the throne of God most high, There flows a living stream;
How musical its dreamy tide, How bright its waters gleam!

Chorus.
Oh, the water of life! It is pure and free,
And it flows thro' the years Of Eternity.

2 The saints of God, forever blest,
Upon its bright banks stand;
By breezes soft and sweetly pure,
Their brows are ever fanned.
Oh, the water of life, etc.

3 They drink from that fair stream of life,
Their earthly toils are past;
They stand within the shining gates,
And heaven is gained at last.
Oh, the water of life, etc.

'TIS RELIGION.

1 'T is religion that can give
Sweetest pleasure while we live;
'T is religion must supply
Solid comfort when we die.

2 After death, its joys will be
Lasting as eternity!
Be the living God my friend,
Then my bliss shall never end.

MY SOUL BE ON THY GUARD.

DR. L. MASON.

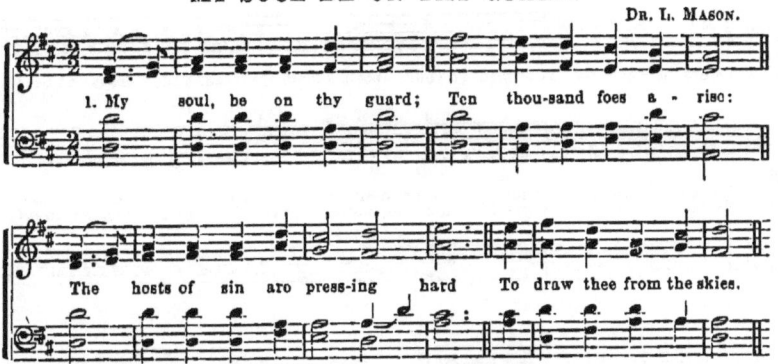

1. My soul, be on thy guard; Ten thousand foes arise: The hosts of sin are pressing hard To draw thee from the skies.

2 O, watch and fight and pray;
The battle ne'er give o'er;
Renew it boldly every day,
And help divine implore.

3 Ne'er think the victory won,
Nor lay thine armor down;
Thy arduous work will not be done
Till thou obtain thy crown.

4 Fight on, my soul, till death
Shall bring thee to thy God;
He'll take thee at thy parting breath,
To his divine abode.

PLEYEL'S HYMN.

J. PLEYEL.

1. Lord, we come before thee now— At thy feet we humbly bow; O, do not our suit disdain! Shall we seek thee, Lord, in vain?

2 Lord, on thee our souls depend;
In compassion now descend;
Fill our hearts with thy rich grace,
Tune our lips to sing thy praise.

3 In thy own appointed way,
Now we seek thee, here we stay;
Lord, we know not how to go,
Till a blessing thou bestow.

4 Send some message from thy word,
That may peace and joy afford;
Let thy Spirit now impart
Full salvation to each heart.

3 Yes, soon will all my pains be past;
My sorrows, gone forever;
And Christ will place upon my brow,
A crown that fadeth never.
I see the angels, etc.

4 Then think not of the mournful time
When dust to dust was given;
But often think of that bright day
When we shall meet in heaven.
I see the angels, etc.

JESUS, LOVER OF MY SOUL.*

Song with Vocal or Chorus Accompaniment.

WM. B. BRADBURY.

NOTE.—This may be used occasionally with fine effect, by one Soprano singing the song, and all the Girls (and Boys whose voices have not changed), singing the Alto, while Base and Tenor sing their respective parts. Such pieces as the above, too difficult, it may be, for general use, are intended for S. S. concerts, and other public performances in which ample time for preparation is allowed. The accompanying parts should be sung in a soft, subdued tone of voice.

*From "Fresh Laurels," published by Biglow & Main, N. Y., by permission.

JESUS, LOVER OF MY SOUL. Concluded.

2 Other refuge have I none,
　Hangs my helpless soul on thee;
　Leave, ah! leave me not alone,
　　Still support and comfort me;
　All my trust on thee is stayed,
　All my help from thee I bring—
　Cover my defenseless head
　　With the shadow of thy wing.

3 Thou, O Christ, art all I want,
　Boundless love in thee I find;
　Raise the fallen, cheer the faint,
　　Heal the sick, and lead the blind.

　Just and holy is thy name,
　Prince of peace and righteousness,
　Most unworthy, Lord, I am—
　　Thou art full of love and grace.

4 Plenteous grace with thee is found—
　Grace to pardon all my sin;
　Let the healing streams abound,
　　Make and keep me pure within.
　Thou of life the fountain art,
　Freely let me take of thee;
　Spring thou up within my heart,
　　Rise to all eternity.

HOSANNA TO JESUS.

J. H. ROSECRANS.

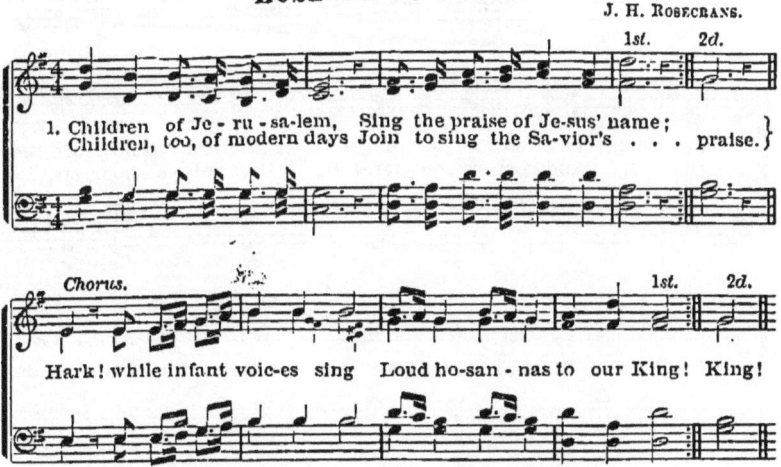

2 We are taught to love the Lord;
　We are taught to read his word;
　We are taught the way to heaven;
　Praise for all to God be given.
　　Hark! while infant, etc.

3 Parents, teachers, old and young,
　All unite to swell the song;
　Higher and yet higher rise,
　Till hosannas reach the skies.
　　Hark! while infant, etc.

CHILDREN SINGING.

Written for this work. Words and Music by BENJ. SKENE.
Sprightly.

1. Sweet hour, on Lord's day morning, The hour the children meet, With best of all adorning, Their faces smiling sweet; Oh, what a happy throng! See! how they join with rapture, To swell the op'ning song. Oh, sweetest hour of the best of days, The hour the children meet To sing the Savior's praise.

2. They sing of Jesus' glory, Glory he had on high, And of the sad, sad story, Of how he came to die. They sing of how he triumphed O'er death, the grave, and sin, And of the golden city, And how he entered in. Oh, sweetest hour, etc.

3 Not in the realms of glory—
Not in the courts above—
Is there a sweeter story
Than that of Jesus' love.
Is love for sinners dying,
A lost and fallen race—
He hears their groans and crying,
And saves them by his grace.
Oh, sweetest hour, etc.

4 Well may we shout our chorus
In praise of Jesus' name,
With those who've gone before us,
To magnify his fame.
Sing on, sing on, dear children,
On earth no sweeter thing
Than these same simple praises,
Which you so sweetly sing.
Oh, sweetest hour, etc.

OH, SEND FORTH THE BIBLE.*

WM. B. BRADBURY.

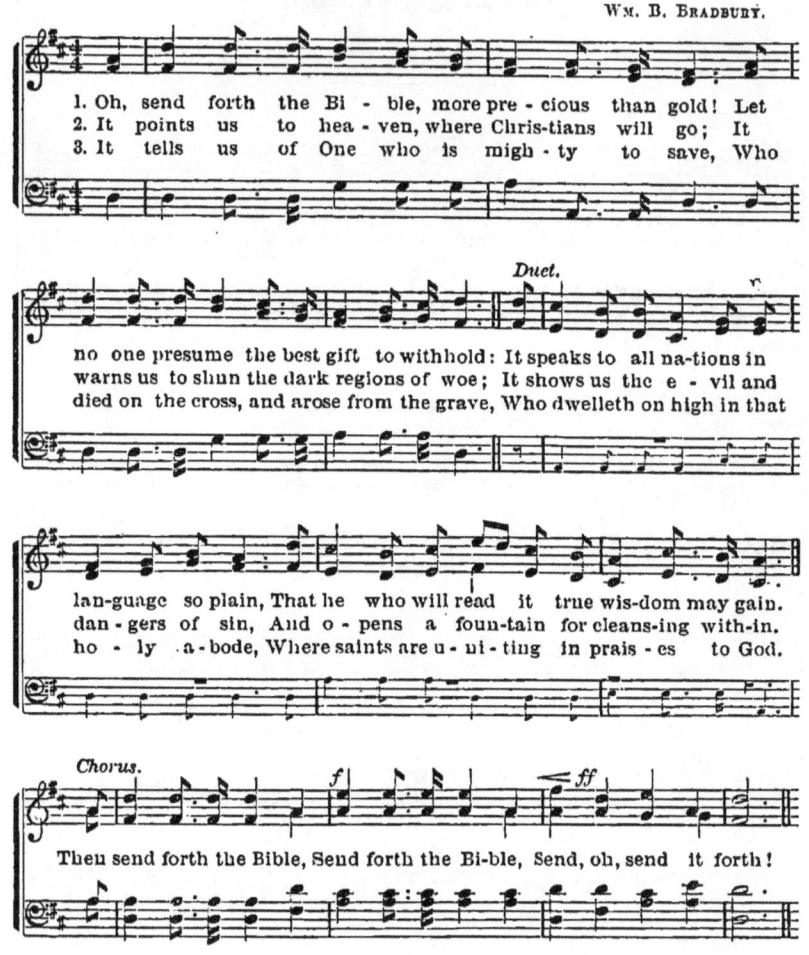

1. Oh, send forth the Bi - ble, more pre - cious than gold! Let no one presume the best gift to withhold: It speaks to all na-tions in lan-guage so plain, That he who will read it true wis-dom may gain.
2. It points us to hea - ven, where Chris-tians will go; It warns us to shun the dark regions of woe; It shows us the e - vil and dan - gers of sin, And o - pens a foun-tain for cleans-ing with-in.
3. It tells us of One who is migh - ty to save, Who died on the cross, and arose from the grave, Who dwelleth on high in that ho - ly a - bode, Where saints are u - ni - ting in prais - es to God.

Chorus. Then send forth the Bible, Send forth the Bi-ble, Send, oh, send it forth!

4 It tells us that all will awake from the tomb;
Bids sinners reflect on a judgment to come;
It tells us that mansions of bliss are prepared,
The hope of believers—their glorious reward.
Then send forth the Bible, etc.

5 Oh, who would neglect such a volume as this,
That warns us from danger, invites us to bliss?
Send forth the blest Bible, earth's regions around,
Wherever the footsteps of man shall be found.
Then send forth the Bible, etc.

* From "Bright Jewels," published by Biglow & Main, N. Y., by permission.

JESUS HAS DIED FOR ME.

"In due time Christ died for the ungodly."

From "Little Sower," by per.   J. H. ROSECRANS.

1. Tho' oft mine eyes with wondering gaze The works of God may see,
No work can e'er with this compare; Jesus has died for me.

2. When burdened with a sense of sin, I to his cross will flee,
And plead for grace and peace with-in, For Jesus died for me.

Chorus.
For Jesus died for me, He groaned up-on the tree;
I dai-ly to his cross will flee, For Jesus died for me.

3 The world may lure me with its smiles,
  Its shallowness I see;
  Its snares shall ne'er my soul beguile,
  Since Jesus died for me.
    For Jesus died, etc.

4 On God I'll cast my every care,
  To him I'll bow the knee;
  To him my every want declare,
  For Jesus died for me.
    For Jesus, etc.

DOXOLOGY.

Praise God, ye heavenly hosts above!
Praise him, all creatures of his love!
Praise him each morning, noon, and night,
Praise him with holy sweet delight.

THE CROWN.

Words by FANNY CROSBY.   C. O. NEVERS.

1. In yon-der ra-diant world a-bove, Where angels sing, and all is love,
2. Shall I the pearl-y gates be-hold, And walk the streets of purest gold?

Where one e-ter-nal sum-mer reigns In beauty o'er the sa-cred plains,
Or on the river's bank repose, Whose stream like murmuring mu-sic flows?

f Chorus.

Is there a crown laid up for me? A beau-ti-ful star-ry
There is a crown laid up for me, A beau-ti-ful star-ry

crown for me? My tri-als o'er, my joy com-plete, Oh,
crown for me. My tri-als o'er, my joys com-plete, Thro'

may I cast at Je-sus' feet, My beau-ti-ful star-ry crown.
grace I'll cast at Je-sus' feet, My beau-ti-ful star-ry crown.

3 Shall I among the angel band,
   A soul redeemed in glory stand?
   And swell with them the choral lay,
   When time itself shall pass away?
   Is there a crown, etc.

4 If here I bear the Christian's part,
   With all the strength of mind and heart,
   My blessed Lord a pledge has given,
   Of rest for me, sweet rest in heaven.
   There is a crown, etc.

*From "Silver Wings," published by O. Ditson & Co., Boston, Mass., by permission.

ONE BY ONE.

"I will give thee a crown of life."—REV. ii: 10.

Mrs. LYDIA BAXTER.   From "Songs of Salvation," T. E. PERKINS, by per.

3 One by one the heavy-laden
   Sink beneath the noontide sun,
  And the aged pilgrim welcomes
   Evening shadows as they come.
One by one, with sins forgiven,

May we stand upon the shore,
  Waiting till the blessed Spirit
Takes our hand and guides us o'er,
  And the loving, gentle Spirit
Leads us to the shining shore.

OUR HOME BY THE RIVER OF LIFE. Concluded.

3 In our beautiful home in the heavenly land,
    The immaculate Lamb is the Light,
And the hosts that have gotten the victory stand
    With the palm and the raiment of white.
At last we shall sit by the side of the stream,
And our loved ones shall be to our souls what they seem,
When our spirits are borne in a rapturous dream
    To our home by the river of life.
        Our home, etc.

THAT GLORIOUS LAND.

From "New Violet," by permission.   Words and Music by A. D. Fillmore.

1. The Bi - ble re - veals a glorious land, Where angels and pu - ri - fied spir-its dwell,
2. Out - gush-ing beneath the throne of God, And of the blest Lamb at his right hand,
3. In the midst of the street on eith-er side, The tree of life arch-ing the way o'ershades,

Where pleasures ne'er end, at God's right hand, And anthems of praises forev - er swell.
Thence run-neth the crystal stream of life, A fountain of joy in that Glo - rious Land.
With health-giving fo - liage far and wide—No sickness this Glorious Land in-vades.

In that Glo-rious Land, what a hap - py band Ere long we shall stand, and

sing with them In the cit - y of God—Je - ru - sa - lem.

4 Twelve manner of fruits hang pendant there,
And all who partake shall never die;
With Jesus they dwell, and ever share
The joys of that Glorious Land on high.
In that Glorious Land, etc.

5 The afflictions of life are brief and light,
While faith looks beyond the dark Jordan's strand,
Where goldenly shine the mansions bright,
Which Jesus prepares in that Glorious Land.
In that Glorious Land, etc.

6 Then come, my dear brethren, let us haste
To finish our work with unfaltering hand,
And soon the sweet joys of heaven we'll taste,
With all the redeemed in that Glorious Land.
In that Glorious Land, etc.

I WILL SING FOR JESUS.

"Making melody in your hearts to your Lord."

By permission. PHILIP PHILLIPS.

1. I will sing for Jesus; With his blood he bought me,
2. Can there o-ver-take me A-ny dark dis-as-ter,

And all a-long my pilgrim way His lov-ing hand has brought me.
While I sing for Je-sus, My bless-ed, bless-ed Mas-ter?

Chorus.

Oh! help me sing for Je-sus, Help me tell the sto-ry
Of him who did re-deem us, The Lord of life and glo-ry.

3 I will sing for Jesus!
  His name alone prevailing,
  Shall be my sweetest music,
    When heart and flesh are failing.
    Oh, help me sing, etc.

4 Still I'll sing for Jesus!
  Oh, how will I adore him,
  Among the cloud of witnesses,
    Who cast their crowns before him.
    Oh, help me sing, etc.

LET THE CHILDREN COME.

Words by B. Skene. M. F. Price.

1. Let the chil-dren come to me, the bless-ed Sav-ior said, While on each he laid his hands with blessings on their head; Je-sus, once himself a child, he loves the children still, And would have them come to him, and dwell on Zion's hill.

2. There, in robes of right-eousness, and with harps of gold-en wires, We will join the angel throng, ten thousand, thousand choirs; Boldly then we'll strike our harps, strike with a fearless hand, Raise our voice, and swell the tones of the bright angelic band.

Chorus.

Let the chil-dren come, Let the chil-dren come; He will guide them home, Home to glo-ry in his Fa-ther's house, Nev-er-more a-gain to roam.

3 Mingling voices, sweetest sounds, with the harp's harmonious chord,
Make the glorious music, meet to praise the blessed Lord;
All that's bright and beautiful, enjoyed in heaven above,
Is secured to children dear, in Jesus' precious love.
    Let the children come, etc.

3 Tell me of heaven, but not of its glory,
Oh, speak of the love that is perfected there;
Tell of the rest that is waiting the weary,
Oh, sing of the home he has gone to prepare.
'Tis not the radiance of sapphire and emerald,
'Tis not the grandeur of heaven's high dome,
None of these things have a tithe of the sweetness
That dwells in the promise of love, rest, and home.
Tell me of heaven, etc.

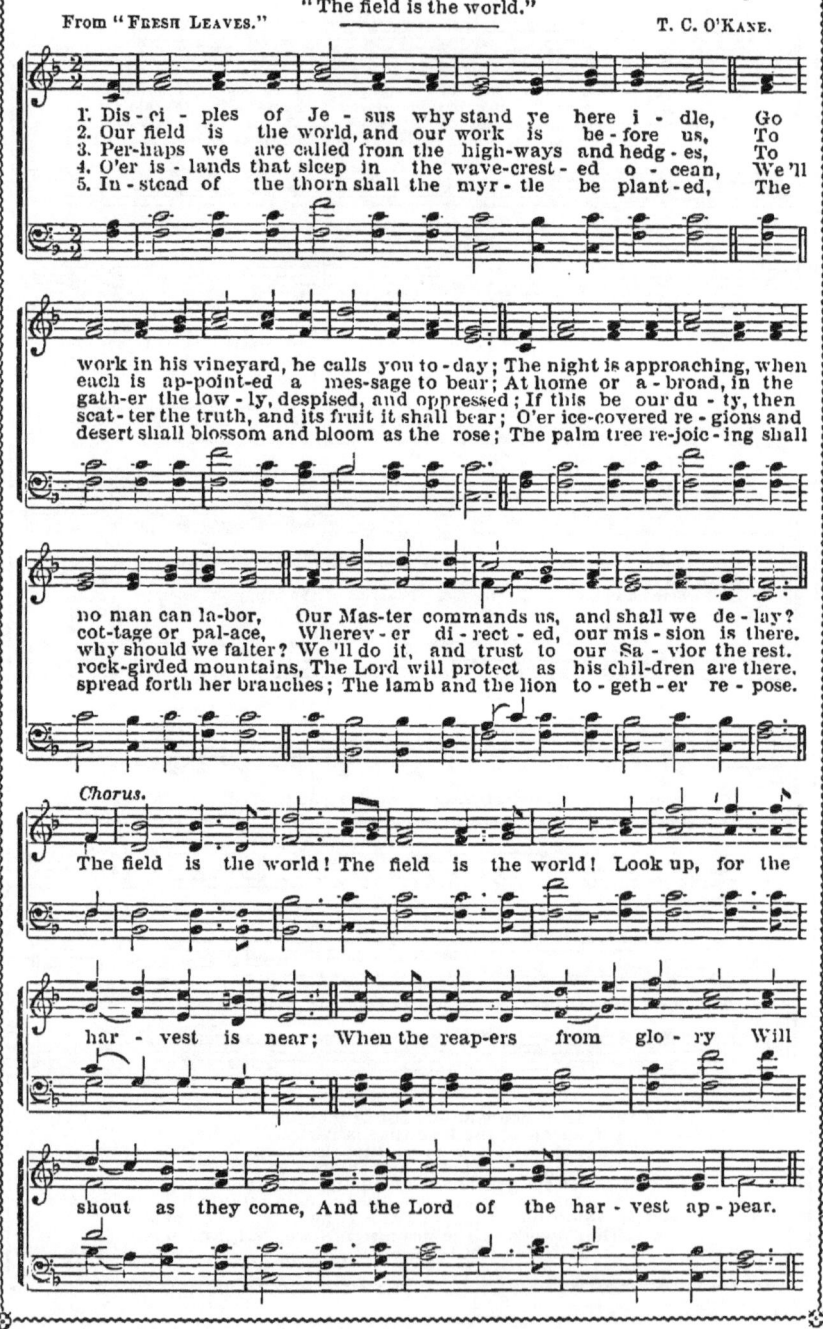

THE CROWN OF MY HOPE.

Specially contributed to this work. J. G. ARCHER.

Joyfully.

1. To Je-sus, the crown of my hope, My soul is in haste to be gone;
Oh, bear me, ye cher-u-bim, up, And waft me a-way to his throne.
My Sav-ior, whom absent, I love; Whom, not having seen, I a-dore;
Whose name is ex-alt-ed a-bove All glo-ry, dominion, and power!

2. Dissolve thou those bands that detain My soul from her portion in thee;
Ah! strike off this ad-amant chain, And make me e-ter-nal-ly free.
When that hap-py e-ra be-gins, When arrayed in thy glories I shine,
Nor grieve a-ny more, by my sins, The bo-som on which I re-cline.

3 Oh then shall the vail be removed!
And round me thy brightness be poured;
I shall meet him whom absent I loved,
I shall see, whom unseen I adored.
And then, nevermore shall the fears,
The trials, temptations, and woes,
Which darken this valley of tears,
Intrude on my blissful repose.

SACRED TEARS.

"Jesus wept."

Words by Mrs. St. Leon Loud. Dr. M. C. Ramsey.

1. Draw near, ye wea-ry, bowed, and broken hearted; Ye on-ward trav'lers to a peace-ful bourne; Ye from whose path the light has all de-part-ed— Ye who in sol-i-tude are left to mourn. Tho' o'er your spir-it hath the storm-cloud swept, Sa-cred are sor-row's tears since "Je-sus wept."

2. The bright and spotless heir of end-less glo-ry, Wept o'er the woes of those he came to save; And an-gels won-dered, when they heard the sto-ry, That he who conquered death wept o'er the grave; For 't was not when his lone-ly watch he kept In dark Geth-se-ma-ne, that "Je-sus wept."

3 But with the friends he loved, whose hope had perished,
The Savior stood, while through his bosom rushed
A tide of sympathy for those he cherished,
And from his eyes the burning tear-drops gushed;
And bending o'er the tomb where Lazarus slept,
In agony of spirit, "Jesus wept."

4 Lo! Jesus' power the sleep of death hath broken,
And wiped the tear from sorrow's drooping eye!
Look up, ye mourners, hear what he hath spoken;
"He that believes on me shall never die!"
Through faith and love your spirits shall be kept;
Sacred are sorrow's tears, since "Jesus wept."

CALL OF THE BELL.

From the "Children's Friend," by A. C. Hopkins.

1. Hark! the deep-toned bell is call-ing, Come! oh, come!
2. Now a-gain its tones are peal-ing, Come! oh, come!

Wea-ry ones, wher-e'er you wan-der, Hith-er come.
In the sa-cred tem-ple kneel-ing, Seek thy home.

Loud-er now, and deep-er peal-ing, On the heart that
Come, and round the al-tar bend-ing, Love the place where

voice is steal-ing, Come, nor lon-ger roam, Come, nor lon-ger roam.
God, de-scend-ing, Calls the spir-it home, Calls the spir-it home.

3 Still the echoed voice is ringing,
    Come! oh, come!
Every heart pure incense bringing,
    Hither come.
Father, round thy footstool bending,
May our souls, to heaven ascending,
    Find in thee their home,
    Find in thee their home.

OH, GIVE ME A HOME.

Words and Music by K. SHAW.

1. Oh, give me a home on that beau-ti-ful shore, Where the sor-rows of life shall come nev-er more; Where we all shall meet, a lov-ing, happy band, And dwell for-ev-er in that beau-ti-ful land.
2. Our Sa-vior has gone to that mansion of rest, To pre-pare us a place to dwell with the blest; We shall see him there on Canaan's golden strand, And sing for-ev-er in that beau-ti-ful land.
3. We have friends gone before who will greet us when we come, And an-gels are there to wel-come us home; Oh, we there shall meet and with our loved ones stand, And praise forever in that beau-ti-ful land.
4. Let us walk in the steps where our ris-en Lord has trod, They will lead us to dwell with children of God; When the warfare's past, with the victor's palm in hand, We'll rejoice forev-er in that beau-ti-ful land.

Chorus.

Oh, say, will you go to that beautiful home, In the land where the glorified ev-er shall roam; With our crowns so bright, and with an-gels we shall stand, And sing for-ev-er in that beau-ti-ful land.

4 If we knew, alas! and do we
  Ever care or seek to know,
Whether bitter herbs or roses
  In our neighbor's garden grow?
Better far along life's pathway,
  Keep this golden rule in view,
"You should always care for others,
  As you'd have them care for you."

ALL ARE FADING.

S. J. Vail.

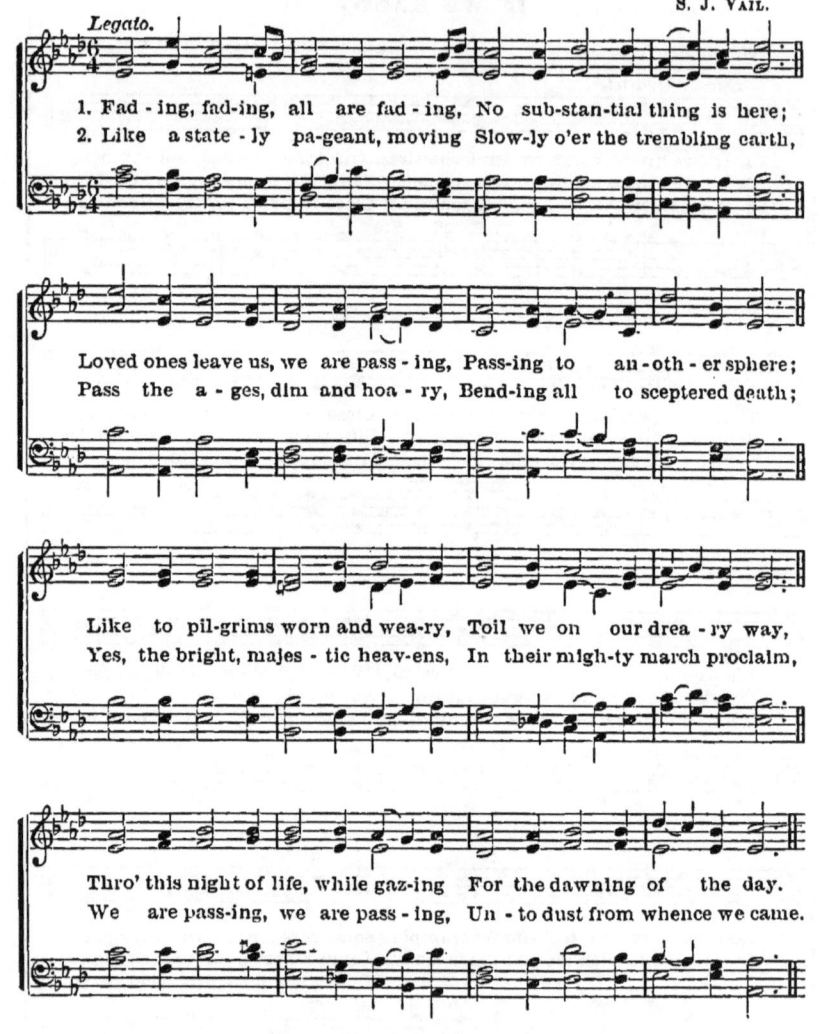

1. Fad-ing, fad-ing, all are fad-ing, No sub-stan-tial thing is here;
Loved ones leave us, we are pass-ing, Pass-ing to an-oth-er sphere;
Like to pil-grims worn and wea-ry, Toil we on our drea-ry way,
Thro' this night of life, while gaz-ing For the dawning of the day.

2. Like a state-ly pa-geant, moving Slow-ly o'er the trembling earth,
Pass the a-ges, dim and hoa-ry, Bend-ing all to sceptered death;
Yes, the bright, majes-tic heav-ens, In their migh-ty march proclaim,
We are pass-ing, we are pass-ing, Un-to dust from whence we came.

3 But when like a baseless vision
All have faded thus away,
There is built a home eternal
For the weary pilgrim's stay.
On the hills of God it standeth,
Rearing high its golden dome,
And the song comes swelling from it,
Welcome, pilgrims, welcome home.

THE RESCUE.

"The Lord also will be a refuge for the oppressed, a refuge in time of trouble."

From "Singing Pilgrim" & "Musical Leaves," by permission of PHILIP PHILLIPS.

1. A ship was on the mighty deep, With all her sails unfurled, Tho' scarce a breath, that calm still morn, The crest-ed billow curled. For many an hour up-on the wave That state-ly ves-sel lay; Then spread her canvass to the breeze, And proudly sailed a-way.
2. Her deck was throng'd with precious souls, The young and old were there, And some with furrowed brows that woke Full man-y a trace of care. They glided on— a week had passed, The sky was still se-rene, As if a storm could nev-er change The beau-ty of the scene.
3. All drank the cup that Pleasure held, But gave no thought to Him, Their heaven'ly guide, whose bounteous hand Had filled it to the brim. But see far off, where yonder sun Is fad-ing to his rest; That bank of clouds portentous rise A-long the golden west!

4. Now peal on peal loud thunders roll, And vivid lightnings flash! And now against the vessel's side The an-gry billows dash!

THE RESCUE. Concluded.

CHILDREN'S ANTHEM.

From the "NEW VIOLET." J. W. SUFFERN.

1. What are those soul-reviving strains, Which echo thus from Salem's plains?
2. Oh, what sweet music, what a song, Sounds from this bright and happy throng!

What anthems loud and loud-er still, So sweetly sound from Zi-on's hill?
Sweet songs whose melting sounds impart Joy to each raptur'd, list'ning heart;

Lo! 'tis an in-fant cho-rus sings Ho-san-na to the King of kings;
Nor these alone their voice shall raise, For we will join this song of praise;

The Savior comes, and babes proclaim Sal-va-tion sent in Je-sus' name.
Still Is-rael's children forward press, To hail the Lord their righteousness.

3 Messiah's name shall joy impart
Alike to Jew and Gentile heart;
He bled for us, he bled for you,
And we will sing hosannas too;
Proclaim hosannas loud and clear:
See David's Son and Lord appear!
All praise on earth to him be given,
And glory shout thro' highest heaven.

FRIEND AFTER FRIEND DEPARTS.

Words by MONTGOMERY. E. McCOY.

1. Friend af-ter friend de-parts; Who hath not lost a friend? There is no un-ion here of hearts, That finds not here an end; Were this frail world our on-ly rest, Liv-ing or dy-ing, none were blest.
2. Be-yond the flight of time, Be-yond this vale of death, There sure-ly is some bless-ed clime Where life is not a breath, Nor life's af-fec-tions transient fire, Whose sparks fly upward to expire.
3. There is a world a-bove, Where part-ing is un-known; A whole e-ter-ni-ty of love, Formed for the good a-lone; And faith beholds the dy-ing here Trans-la-ted to that happier sphere.

4 Thus star by star declines,
  Till all are passed away,
As morning high and higher shines
  To pure and perfect day.
Nor sink those stars in empty night,
They hide themselves in heaven's own light.

ALTOGETHER LOVELY.

1 Jesus, I love thy charming name,
  'T is music to my ear;
Fain would I sound it out so loud,
  That all the earth might hear.

2 Yes, thou art precious to my soul,
  My transport and my trust;
Jewels to thee are gaudy toys,
  And gold is sordid dust.

3 All that my ardent soul can wish,
  In thee doth richly meet;
Nor to my eyes is light so dear,
  Nor friendship half so sweet.

4 I'll speak the honors of thy name
  With my last laboring breath,
And, dying, triumph in thy cross,
  The antidote of death.

JESUS AT THE WELL.

Words by Rev. E. G. Taylor.*
A. Rosecrans.

1. There's a beau-ti-ful sto-ry the Scrip-tures tell, Of Je-sus our Lord, as he sat on the well, In the cit-y of Sy-char, and taught his sweet law, To a woman who came there the water to draw. She knew not the stranger, nor e-ven could think 'T was Je-sus, who said to her, "Give me to drink;"

2. Oh, sweet were the wa-ters which came from the well, Where the Sa-vior sat down as the Scrip-tures tell, But sweet-er, and dear-er, and pu-rer are they Which flow from the wells of Salvation to-day; For Jesus declared, as he sat on the brink Of the well of Sa-ma-ria, "Whoev-er shall drink

3. Of Je-sus, our Mas-ter, who sat on the well, And taught this poor wo-man, thy sto-ry we'll tell, To all who will lis-ten, how free thou dost give Sal-vation's bright waters to all who will live. And grant that, like her's, our pe-ti-tion may be—"Lord, give us this wa-ter, so sweet and so free,"

*Words from the "Sunday-School Teacher," by permission.

JESUS AT THE WELL. Concluded.

But quick-ly she learned it was Christ—it was he Who gives of the wa-ter of life so free. The wa-ter of life, so sweet, so free, Is flow-ing for all, for you, for me; And Christ is the giv-er, the Scriptures tell, Our Lord who sat on Ja-cob's well.

Of the wa-ter that I for the world have in store, A well have in him, and thirst never-more." The wa-ter, etc.

That wells of sal-va-tion may in us be found, To spring up to life, and ev-er a-bound. The wa-ter, etc.

WILL YOU GO?

1 We're trav'ling home to heaven above,
   Will you go?
To sing the Savior's dying love,
   Will you go?
Millions have reached that blest abode,
Anointed kings and priest to God,
And millions more are on the road,
   Will you go?

2 We're going to see the bleeding Lamb,
   Will you go?
In rapturous strains to praise his name,
   Will you go?
The crown of life we there shall wear,
The conqueror's palms our hands shall bear,
And all the joys of heaven we'll share,
   Will you go?

3 We're going to join the heavenly choir,
   Will you go?
To raise our voice and tune the lyre,
   Will you go?
There saints and angels gladly sing
Hosanna to their God and King,
And make the heavenly arches ring,
   Will you go?

4 The way to heaven is straight and plain,
   Will you go?
Believe, repent, be born again,
   Will you go?
The Savior cries aloud to thee,
"Take up thy cross, and follow me,
And thou shalt my salvation see,
   Come to me."

ROBED IN WHITE.

Words by Mrs. M. R. Butler.
Benj. Skene.

1. One who loved the Sav-ior best, Told a sto-ry, strange and true, Of a "Cit-y of the Blest" Out of mor-tal reach or view, Where God's chil-dren, robed in white, Wan-der in his lov-ing sight.
2. On, through "shin-ing streets of gold," In-to jew-eled pal-ace homes, Where no dark-ness, storm, or cold, And no sun-light ev-er comes; But "the Fa-ther giv-eth light" Where his chil-dren walk in white.
3. But if here our spir-its are Soiled or stained by earth and sin, Though the gates of pearl un-bar, We shall nev-er en-ter in; Nev-er, nev-er walk in white, Through the shin-ing streets of light.

4 Only hands as pure as snow,
Only feet that stainless trod,
Only sinless spirits go
To the "City of our God."
Where sweet children walk in white,
In the Father's loving sight.

JUST BEYOND.

Words by Mrs. B. J. BITTLE. K. SHAW.

3 Just beyond, though seeming far,
  Just beyond, just beyond;
  Though our trials heavy are,
  Just beyond, just beyond
  Many mansions waiting stand,
  Nearing now the silver strand;
  Soon we'll reach the better land,
  Just beyond, just beyond.

4 Just beyond, deliverance lies,
  Just beyond, just beyond;
  One step only, and we rise,
  Just beyond, just beyond,
  Unto pure, undying love,
  Unto friends death can't remove;
  Unto peace, all thought above,
  Just beyond, just beyond.

FAR BEYOND.

Words and Music by K. Shaw.

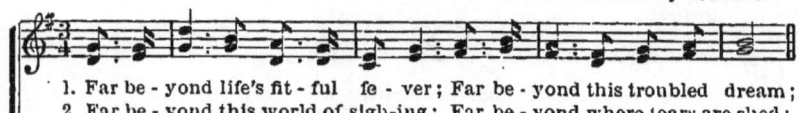

1. Far be-yond life's fit-ful fe-ver; Far be-yond this troubled dream;
2. Far be-yond this world of sigh-ing; Far be-yond where tears are shed;
3. Far be-yond these painful partings; Far be-yond these bit-ter tears;

Far be-yond cold Jor-dan's riv-er; Far be-yond that sul-len stream;
Far be-yond the skies and dy-ing; Far be-yond the mold-'ring dead;
Far be-yond these weary heart-aches; Far beyond these hopes and fears;

Chorus.

There we'll meet to part, no, never! There we'll roam the gold-en shore,

Where the liv-ing life for-ev-er, And the sun goes down no more.

4 Oh, that home beyond the shadows!
   That dear land we soon shall gain;
   Where we'll meet the blessed Savior,
   Free from sorrow, toil, and pain.
       There we'll meet, etc.

5 Blessed Savior, help us daily,
   While we're here on earthly ground;
   Help us walk in wisdom's pathway,
   To that world that's far beyond.
       There we'll meet, etc.

WE'LL DO ALL THAT WE CAN.

"The time is short."

From "FRESH LEAVES," by permission.
T. C. O'KANE.

1. We nev-er will think there is naught we can do, Be-cause we can't work like a man, The har-vest is great, and the lab-'rers are few, So we must do all that we can.
2. And if we have on-ly a pen-ny to give, We'll give it, though scanty our store; For they who give nothing when lit-tle they have, When weal-thy will give lit-tle more.
3. But if an a-bun-dance we have at com-mand, O Fa-ther! the spir-it be-stow, To scat-ter our wealth with a lib-er-al hand, To cheer those in sor-row and woe.

Chorus.

Oh, yes, we'll do all that we can, Oh, yes, we'll do all that we can; The harvest is great and the lab'rers are few, So we must do all that we can.

Ritard.

4 Though God may not call us in regions afar,
To scatter the gospel abroad,
We'll point those around us to Bethlehem's star,
To heaven, to home, and to God.
Oh yes, we'll do all, etc.

5 For Jesus our Savior, our talents, and time,
And money, we'll cheerfully spend;
Whatever our station, wherever our clime,
We'll serve him, and love to the end.
Oh yes, we'll do all, etc.

BETHANY.

"Though he be not far from every one of us."—ACTS xvii: 27.

Dr. L. MASON.

1. Near-er, my God, to thee, Near-er to thee! E'en tho' it
2. Tho' like the wan-der-er, The sun gone down, Dark-ness be
3. There let the way ap-pear Steps un-to heaven, All that thou

be a cross That rais-eth me! Still all my song shall be,
o-ver me, My rest a stone, Yet in my dreams I'd be
send-est me, In mer-cy given; An-gels to beck-on me,

Near-er, my God, to thee, Near-er, my God, to thee, Near-er to thee.

4 Then with my waking thoughts,
   Bright with thy praise,
   Out of my stony griefs
   Bethel I'll raise;
   So by my woes to be
   Nearer, my God, to thee,
   Nearer to thee.

5 Or if, on joyful wing,
   Cleaving the skies,
   Sun, moon, and stars forgot,
   Upward I fly,
   Still all my song shall be,
   Nearer, my God, to thee,
   Nearer to thee.

OUR FATHER. Chant.

"After this manner pray ye."—MATT. vi: 9.

TALLIS.

1. Our Father who art in heaven, hallowed | be thy | name;
   Thy kingdom come; thy will be done, on | earth...as it | is in | heaven.
2. Give us this day our | daily | bread;
   And forgive us our trespasses, as we forgive | them that | trespass a- | gainst us.
3. And lead us not into temptation, but deliver | us from | evil;
   For thine is the kingdom, and the power, and the glory, for- | ever..and | ever.
   |A- | men.

CHARITY THINKETH NO EVIL.

KNOWLES SHAW.

1. Oh, be not the first to dis-cov-er A flaw in the fame of a friend;
A fault in the faith of a bro-ther, Whose heart may be true to the end;
A hint or a nod may a-wa-ken Sus-pi-cion most false and un-true;
And thus our be-lief may be sha-ken In those who are hon-est and true.

2. How of-ten the sigh of de-jec-tion Is heard from the hyp-ocrite's breast,
To par-o-dy truth and af-fec-tion, Or lull a sus-pi-cion to rest;
And of-ten the light smile of glad-ness Is worn by the friends that we meet,
To cov-er a soul full of sad-ness, Too proud to acknowledge de-feat.

3 Leave base minds to harbor suspicion,
   And low ones to trace out defects;
Let ours be a nobler ambition,
   For base is the mind that suspects.
For often the friends we hold dearest,
   Their noblest emotions conceal;
For bosoms the purest, sincerest,
   Have thoughts they can never reveal.

THE LAND CELESTIAL.

Words by Fanny Church. From "Little Sower." J. H. Rosecrans.

1. There is a land ce-les-tial, A world that's bright and fair;
   There flows the peaceful riv-er, Beneath the tree of life,
   And o'er its ho-ly beau-ty, Floats not a cloud of care;
   There comes no wail of mourn-ing, Nor sound of bit-ter strife.

Chorus.
Land of per-fect beau-ty, World so bright and fair,
When will an-gels call me, When shall I be there?

2 There are the sweet-voiced angels,
   Around the great white throne,
Who bow in willing homage
   To him who rules alone.
Death guards the mystic portals,
   And gently one by one
He leads in weary mortals,
   Whose earthly work is done.
      Land of, etc.

3 They stand before the Father,
   The Lord of life and love;
He smiles upon his children,
   He welcomes them above.
And all in joyous singing,
   And peace for evermore,
There in that far-off country,
   Upon that golden shore.
      Land of, etc.

LET US LOVE EACH OTHER MORE.

Words by W. S. WINFIELD.   KNOWLES SHAW.

1. Pressing af - ter Christ our Sav-ior, In the path he trod be - fore,
2. Let us bear our brother's bur-den, As our grief the Sav - ior bore;
3. When we've passed the pearly portal, When we've gained that lovely shore,

That we all may grow in fa - vor, Let us love each oth - er more;
Let us cheer the hea - vy - la - den, Let us love each oth - er more;
When we gain the land im - mor-tal, Shall we love each oth - er more?

Sweetest friendships ev - er seek-ing, Pass-ing ev - ery tres-pass o'er,
Let our hearts with kindness glowing, Strive the wanderer to re - store;
Soon we hope to meet in heav-en, Whither now our spir - its soar;

Let us cease from e - vil speaking, Let us love each oth - er more.
Sweet compas-sion ev - er showing, Let us love each oth - er more.
There the Savior's full-ness giv - en, We shall love each oth - er more.

Chorus.

Let us love each oth - er, Let us love each oth-er, Let us love each oth-er, Let us love each oth-er more.

Cho. to 3d verse. We shall love each oth-er, We shall love each oth-er, We shall love each other, We shall love each other more.

GOOD NIGHT TILL THEN.

K. Shaw.

1. I journey forth rejoicing, From this dark vale of tears,
To heavenly joy and freedom, From earthly cares and fears;
Where Christ, our Lord, shall gather All his redeemed again,
His kingdom to inherit. Good night, till then.
Good night, good night, till then.

2. Why thus so sadly weeping, Beloved ones of my heart?
The Lord is good and gracious, Tho' now he bids us part.
Oft have we met in gladness, And we shall meet again,
Set free from every sadness. Good night, till then.

3 I go to see our Savior,
  Whom we have loved below;
To see the blessed angels,
  The holy saints to know;
Our dearest friends departed,
  I go to find again,
And wait for you to join us.
  Good-night, till then.

4 I hear the Savior calling—
  The joyful hour has come;
The angels, too, are ready
  To guide me to our home,
Where Christ our Lord shall gather
  All his redeemed again—
His kingdom to inherit.
  Good night, till then.

LISTEN TO THE WORDS OF JESUS.

Words and Music by BENJ. SKENE.

Not too fast.

1. In our Sun-day school we glad-ly meet, And here each oth-er kind-ly greet; With Ma-ry at the Mas-ter's feet, We lis-ten to the words of Je-sus!

2. For the Sa-vior's words teach wis-dom's ways— The path to take thro' all our days, That we may gain the Mas-ter's praise, We lis-ten to the words of Je-sus!

Chorus. p

Lis-ten, lis-ten, lis-ten to the words of Je-sus.

3 The sinner's way we all must shun;
A race is set for us to run;
To keep the course we have begun,
We listen to the words of Jesus.
Listen! listen, etc.

4 Oh, blessed Savior, give us grace;
May we all see thy smiling face;
Our home be in thy dwelling-place,
And listen to the words of Jesus.
Listen! listen, etc.

3 Work, for the night is coming,
Under the sunset skies;
While their red tints are glowing,
Work, for daylight flies.
Work till the last beam fadeth,
Fadeth to shine no more;
Work while the night is dark'ning,
When man's work is o'er.

THE SHINING RIVER.

Words by J. C. JOHNSON.   From "Little Sower."   A. N. JOHNSON.

1. Don't you hear the an-gels sing By the shin-ing riv-er?
2. Don't you hear the wa-ters flow In the shin-ing riv-er?
3. Don't you hear the an-gels sing By the shin-ing riv-er?

Lil-ies white and ro-ses bring—These are ours for-ev-er.
E'er a-bun-dant, crys-tal, clear—These are ours for-ev-er.
Song, and harp, and gol-den crown—These are ours for-ev-er.

Chorus.

These are in the bet-ter land, There with rap-ture we shall stand,
Soft-ly past the verdant shore, Glide the bil-lows ev-er-more;
Oh, that fragrant, hap-py land, There with rap-ture we shall stand;

Crowned with flowers, immor-tal, rare—These are ours for-ev-er.
Shore and crys-tal wave we view—These are ours for-ev-er.
Flowers and stream, and crown and harp—These are ours for-ev-er.

COME, HUMBLE SINNER.

1 Come, humble sinner, in whose breast
  A thousand thoughts revolve;
  Come, with your guilt and fear oppressed,
  And make this last resolve:

2 I'll go to Jesus, though my sin
  Has like a mountain rose;
  His kingdom now I'll enter in,
  Whatever may oppose.

3 Humbly I'll bow at his command,
  And there my guilt confess;

  I'll own I am a wretch undone
  Without his sovereign grace.

4 Surely he will accept my plea,
  For he has bid me come;
  Forthwith I'll rise, and to him flee,
  For yet, he says, there's room.

5 I can not perish if I go;
  I am resolved to try;
  For if I stay away, I know
  I must forever die.

PRAISE THE LORD.

Words and Music by B. Skene.

1. Praise the Lord! ye saints a-dore him, All u-nite with one ac-cord,
2. Praise the Lord! who ev-ery blessing On our heads hath richly poured,

Bring your off-'rings, come be-fore him— Oh, praise the Lord,
Sing a-loud, his love con-fess-ing— Oh, praise the Lord,

Bring your off'rings, come before him, Oh, praise the Lord!
Sing a-loud, his love con-fess-ing, Oh, praise the Lord!

Praise the Lord!

3 Praise the Lord! who would not praise him?
He hath us to grace restored;
To the highest honors raise him—
Oh, praise the Lord!

4 Praise the Lord! your songs excelling
Worldly music's richest chord;
Sing—your Savior's glory telling—
Oh, praise the Lord!

5 In that world of light and glory,
We shall all, with one accord,
Meet to sing redemption's story—
Oh, praise the Lord!

www.ingramcontent.com/pod-product-compliance
Lightning Source LLC
Chambersburg PA
CBHW032246080426
42735CB00008B/1031